EDEN AND EASTER

EDEN
AND
EASTER

by

Anthony T. Padovano

PAULIST PRESS
New York / Paramus / Toronto

105817

Library of Congress
Catalog Card Number: 73-91370

ISBN: 0-8091-1810-6

Published by Paulist Press
Editorial Office: 1865 Broadway, N.Y., N.Y. 10023
Business Office: 400 Sette Drive, Paramus, N.J. 07652

Printed and bound in the
United States of America

CONTENTS

CREATION AND CHRIST

EASTER AND CHRIST

CREATION AND CHRIST

1

THE GRACE
AND LIGHT
OF CREATION

When a Christian speaks of creation, he refers, not to Nature's beginning but to Revelation's first moment. The beginning of a relationship, not the start of the world, gives creation its religious value. God is not glorified in the existence of matter nor in its development. His glory is achieved, his identity made real, in the bonds of reciprocal love which allow him to offer love and receive its response. The Christian theology of creation remains incomplete when we separate it from a theology of Christ and a theology of community. We shall attempt to restore the harmony of these complementary themes.

The doctrine of the Trinity declares relationship as the crucial element in divine and human life. In the long course of religious history, Christians alone define God essentially in terms of relationship. God cannot be God unless the Father relates to the Son and until that relationship continues into the love of the Spirit. In God, every relationship becomes a person: there are three persons because there are three relationships. If God could not relate, he would cease to exist. Other religions define God as power or intelligence or beauty. Christians define him as the one who relates in order to be.

If creation is made in the image of God, this relational dimension gives creation its meaning. Creation has no religious value when presented as a geographical or cosmic event. Even today, when there is impressive information about physical and biological origins, men turn to Genesis rather than geophysics to grasp the significance of these events and to relate to them humanly. We do not intend to diminish the urgency and necessity of the scientific enterprise. We are stressing the need to perceive the dignity of the creative process in relational terms.

We are haunted by the words which tell of the making of the world, its innocence, the invitation to friendship with God, the dialogue between man and the Creator. These realities evoke human experiences and longings not summoned forth by other data or disciplines of knowledge. This occurs despite the scientific unreliability of Genesis.

The world was not made in seven days nor in the order presented in the Genesis account. Even if the world were made in that time span and sequence, however, we would misuse Scripture if we went to it for that type of knowing. One reads Genesis to establish or re-enforce a relationship, not to discern the physical structures or chemical processes of the universe. The Christian interpretation of creation, therefore, is unrevealed until Genesis is comprehended in the light of the Easter experience, or the first seven days in the light of the Pentecost event. The relationship proclaimed in Genesis is complemented by Christ and the community which derives from him.

There is more than rhetoric, indeed a profound biblical and theological truth, in interpreting the creation of the sun in the action of the breaking of the bread or in continuing the making of the waters in the offer of new wine. Symbolically and really, the seven days of Genesis are linked with the three days of Passover. The Eucharistic Presence and the Creative Spirit of Genesis cannot be isolated from each other.

It is not the Fall of man but the agony of love in a creating God which we behold in the crucifixion of Jesus. It is not only a return to life but a return to the birth of the stars and the first day of the first spring which one perceives in Easter.

The dialogue of creation is extended beyond the relationship of Christ and the Father into a relationship between God and ourselves. The point of creation is not the making of the world but the beginning of a community. God's creative power is the power for community. This is God's most significant work because God is a community. Christianity is distinctive. No other religion defines God as a community. The Father has a Word from the beginning and relates in Love in order to be.

We do not cite the uniqueness of Christianity as a declaration of difference from other religions but as a contribution for dialogue. At some future moment, the three major religions may converge. All religions of world-wide significance derive from Hinduism, Buddhism, and Judaeo-Christianity. The Hindu speaks most pointedly of God as Father, the Judaeo-Christian, of God as Word or Son, the Buddhist, of God as Spirit. The Trinitarian unity of the great religions promises community in the future. The more effective the community which reads it, the greater the meaning of Genesis. The difference Christianity makes should lead to the establishment of similarity with others.

All subsequent history lives out and completes the meaning of the first day of creation. The first day of creation is the first day of Christ and the first day of human community. There remains an unbreakable bond between Creation and Christmas, between the giving of light and the raising of Christ, between the Spirit over the waters and the Pentecost Spirit of community. Creation and community are the same process.

God is a need to be loved. This need is present in the Trinity where identity takes the form of other persons. Creation extends God's need to be loved into his need to be loved by us. Jesus reveals who God is, his need to be loved, his appeal not to be forgotten. The substance of Easter is the need Christ experiences of returning to the disciples. Community is the need we have for one another. When this is related to the need God has for us a community of faith commences.

Creation is grace rather than the molding of matter. Genesis requires for its understanding the grace of God's need for us and the experience of significant relationship. When persons realize a need for one another, this need is grace. When we allow this need to conceive new life, this need becomes creative. The offer of this love to the response of another makes love a redemptive sacrifice, freeing us for transfiguration.

God felt a need for us, yet mysteriously remains sovereign in the same way that submission in love means also to reign. This is the power behind the creative process. In Christ, this love is placed at the disposal of our response so that Calvary and Easter may become a redemptive sacrifice freeing us for transformation. In our need for one another, in the life we give one another, in the love we place at the disposal of one another, we become the image of God, the disciples of Christ, and a community in the Spirit.

2
CREATION
AND COMMUNITY

When a Christian confesses God as Creator, he declares that the only God he knows is the God who creates. Whether there could have been a God who did not create is a question for philosophical inquiry rather than theological reflection. Theology addresses itself to the concrete religious situation. This situation is one which knows God as Creator and knows of no other God.

Creation is more than an invitation by God that we might be involved in his destiny and his life. It is a commitment by God to our destiny and our life. No one is committed on the level of abstraction. One is either concrete in his commitment, or else uncommitted. One cannot be committed to mankind unless he is committed to individual people; one cannot be committed to God unless committed to a particular, definable God; one is not committed to Christ unless he is committed in a specific manner.

In creation, God commits himself in a concrete way. There is nothing vague about creation. Nonetheless, the identity of this creating God remains relatively obscure until God's Son is sacrificed and glorified as Christ. This Event clarifies what creation is for and with what love creation was begun. In Christ, the creating God is revealed as a saving God whose power is less at issue in creation than the limitless character of redemptive love and divine compassion. Genesis and the Gospel provide an insight into power expressing itself as mercy. God's creative Word is uttered fully in Christ where creation and redemption are simultaneously at issue and harmoniously united. Christ is God's act of fidelity to the promise of creation. Christ is constituted not only Lord of salvation but Lord of creation.

The life of Jesus reveals how power and authority can be used in favor of need. In Jesus, God is drawn concretely to our side where he demonstrates the illusionary character of power when divorced from need. Before Pilate, Jesus refers to the fact that power and truth must exist together: "Surely you know I have power to release you and I have power to crucify you?" "You would have no power over me," replied Jesus, "if it had not been given you from above...." (John 19, 10-11). When power crucifies truth, power itself is immobilized. Creation is a revelation of power yielding to life, of power become a redemptive experience. If it is true, as we have said above, that creation is revelation's first moment rather than nature's beginning, it is also true that the goal of creation is not the world but man as a person in community. The purpose of creation is not the evolutive perfection of the cosmos but the development of human personality. A Christian becomes an integral part of the creative process only when he builds community. Nothing engages man more deeply or involves him more fully than the creation of community. Creation reveals God as a community of persons involved in building community with us. The meaning of the creation story is declared in concrete community. Eve is given to Adam as the first expression of human community. The Fall is described as tragic because it shatters the communion between God and Adam, between Adam and Eve, later, between Cain and Abel. The interest of

the creating God centers on the community
which emerges from this creation. Man is allowed to name the animals but communion with
persons, divine and human, is his most urgent
responsibility.

The doctrine of creation orients a Christian
toward power in a distinctive manner. Nothing
is more pagan than the naked pursuit of power.
Man is not made for dominion but for dialogue.
He is made to yield as well as to overcome. The
illusion of power is that somehow this dialogue
is not necessary. Power may give one the impres-
sion that one may dictate rather than discuss. It
holds such a man hostage and makes a prisoner
of someone who imagines himself a captor. Insecurity and power usually exist in direct proportion and as correlative to each other.

The story of creation reveals that the first
use of power is the creation of life. It also reveals
that God, defined as first in power, yields his
power for the sake of communion. The Fall is
not the result of resistance to divine dominion
but the inevitable consequence of a rejection of
persons. It is not the tree of knowledge or a ser-
pentine suggestion but a refusal to abide in
fidelity with persons which destroys Eden.

The life of Jesus sheds further light on the
creation event. Jesus gains power as he surren-

ders power as dominion. He asserts himself by yielding. Power in the service of mercy requires sacrifice and death. This is the authority Jesus reveals. Later, when St. Paul speaks of power or dominion in marriage, he describes the vocation of a husband as a vocation of sacrificing himself for his wife. He compares this with the love Christ demonstrated for the Church over which he had authority. "Husbands should love their wives just as Christ loved the Church and sacrificed himself for her. . . . In the same way, husbands must love their wives. . . ." (Ephesians 5, 25 and 28).

It is the powerless who prevail. The Christian community is characterized by the crucified Christ, Mary of Nazareth, Francis of Assisi, or with a man named John who transformed the power of the papacy into an act of mercy. In the short run, power seems to grant dominion as death, at first sight, seems to have dominion. But love is always a question of yielding. And love is the only thing men really remember.

Creation and the death on the cross are sacraments of yielding and sacrifice. Each is an act of communion and an invitation to community. Each is an act of mercy when power might have been preferred. The Incarnation and the first dawn are symbols of divine compassion, signs of concrete mercy, and, therefore, enlighten history.

The creation account is marked with power for life and forgiveness in distress. Jesus expresses the same meaning in his flesh. From his existence, life and forgiveness follow. In the breaking of the bread, power and mercy are wedded. The promise of redemption in Eden resonates as mercy in the central parable of Jesus. This mercy reaches a decisive expression on the cross when the Son yields to the Father and destroys forever the notion of power as a valid Christian choice.

The message of creation has an especial meaning for American culture. Americans instinctively fear the vastness and mystery of creation. We seek to take its measure or to dominate it by the force of our will. In other words, we wish to overcome our finiteness by dominating our environment. This, it seems to me, was the sin of Adam. The seduction of the tree of knowledge is the temptation of taking rather than yielding for the sake of salvation. Some use the exploration of space or the escalation of the arms race as an act of dominion. In the fruit of technology they reach for the power by which they might be made gods. The story of creation alerts us to the fact that man achieves his transformation not by a dominion of his environment but by responsibility to himself and others. Without giving, it has been said, receiving is empty; without receiving, giving is domination. God yields his life in creation; this mercy allows the power to bestow life. Christ yields his life on the cross; from this mercy comes the power to heal life. Only the person who yields to another can enter into communion with him. They alone have power with us who demonstrate their love in mercy.

Because Christ is at issue in the development of human personhood, it is Christ who is increased and enriched as the world becomes more personal. Christ can only emerge in community. Community is, therefore, the one place for Christians to be; power for communion is the one power allowed a Christian. Creation begins Christ because it situates human life in a communal experience and unites power to the capacity for mercy. It is Satan who suggests that creation is for dominion and power, for isolated supremacy. Creation is marred by the Fall whenever Cain dominates; it renews itself in the blood of Abel or of Christ, in the yielding of Abraham and in the surrender of the cross. Creation is, therefore, a paradox and a challenge. It happens when God asserts himself by giving himself away. In a sense, this self-donation is the only thing which has ever really happened in history.

3
EVOLUTION
AND SELF-REVELATION

A doctrine of creation is not limited to a consideration of God as Creator. We sense in the core of our being a kinship with the earth. The earth is not only the place where we live; it is, to some extent, our creator. Man emerges from the earth biologically and psychologically. We are bound to the earth by ties more effective than gravity. Man will never be defined except in terms of the soil and earth, the chemistry and grain, the water and air of this planet. Martin Heidegger's philosophy stresses most effectively man's ontological affinity with the world. Man is *da-sein,* a "being-in-the-world." He cannot be except in the world. He has not been able to be elsewhere nor will he ever be elsewhere unless he is properly situated in a mundane setting. In his essence, man is earth-bound. The nature of the earth which has become inseparable from human nature is evolutive. It is necessary to consider the implications of this fact.

The problem evolution presented to science and religion during the last century has been instructive. Evolution seemed to imply a rejection of the creation account in Genesis and even of biblical truth itself. There was no easy way to disengage the scientific state of the question from a denial of the Scriptures and of God. The clash of opinions was necessary and instructive. It was necessary because both sides approached the truth with misconceptions. It was instructive because each side came to appreciate its own identity and the contribution of the other.

Scientists learned from the controversy the need to refrain from unwarranted theological conclusions. Some scientists had employed scientific data to bolster notions which were theological nonsense. Religious spokesmen learned the importance of allowing science to speak fully and freely before a theological judgment is made concerning possible ramifications in doctrine or practice. Many in the Church were unable or unwilling to consider God or creation in dynamic and evolutive terms. People tended to orate against each other neither listening nor growing in the process. Fear of the real truth prevailed, as it always does when people stop hearing one another.

Evolution is a sacrament of the unity at work in the world. The Scriptures reveal this unity from the vantage point of the one God who creates differently rather than from the vantage point of the creative process. The world is unified because one God is responsible for it, because the world is accountable to him, because the world fulfills his purpose, declares his glory, ends in his love.

Two aspects of this mystery were unclear until evolution became a framework within which to view the world. God seemed to be directly responsible for almost everything. Each reality in the creation account is a result of his explicit action. Evolution highlights the fact that we creatures are responsible for one another in terms of the life we give and even of the structure that life assumes. In other words, creation is unified from within. Evolution explores the inner mystery of this unity proclaimed externally by the Scriptures and from the vantage point of God. Evolution focuses on the derivations, consequences, and relationships of creatures among themselves. The Scriptures proclaim creation as a symbol or sacrament of God's love. Evolution makes it possible to envision creation as a symbol or sacrament of God's unity. Life emerges from life; when it takes on new forms it remains intrinsically homogeneous. The relationship between primitive forms of life, unicellular life or vegetative life, and the highest forms of life, primates and man, is unbreakable. No life in the world is a total stranger to the other.

If we knew the key, the brotherhood and kinship between man and all that lives could be fashioned into harmony. The care of the earth, the Franciscan spirit, the ecological imperative are responses to this mystery. Even the brutal survival of the fittest tells us that no one has life only for himself and that life, like love, must sometimes be given or taken in the agonizing reach upward. By this, we do not mean to justify the evil and exploitative taking of life but to point out how the world finds a way to live through the death which is inseparable from the progress of the world. The seed dies in the earth; man lives from the death of that which nourishes him.

Evolution obliges us to recognize in all forms of life the features of our own life. It calls us to respect and reverence the straining of life for more life in a blade of grass searching for the sunlight or in a tree reaching for air to breathe or in a flight of birds toward the clouds. It asks us to sense the hunger and thirst for more life in the human heart. It invites us to reflect on what it is man must reach for if he, too, is to have life and have it more abundantly.

We are trying to suggest the possibility of operating in an evolutionary perspective for the development of an ascetism of life or a mysticism of life.

As the evolutionary question is discussed with regard to the origins of life in the world and the beginnings of man, we must remain aware that evolution is not a cosmological problem but a way of life. Someone who takes evolution seriously maintains that growth and change are positive values and that perfection or stability is unattainable and undesirable. This insight has implications for a theology of Christ and even for a definition of God. For us, it means that improvement rather than perfection is the objective of spiritual life and moral growth. One never becomes all he should be or all he can be. New life is always possible where man is concerned, even in death. An immediate encounter with God may destine man to continual progress toward God rather than situating him permanently. Salvation is everlasting improvement with no fear of ultimate failure rather than a static although beatific experience.

Human history is an evolutive, changing, aspiring history. Christ is Savior, Lord of history, not because he cannot fail but because he does not fail in his striving. Jesus is a human accomplishment as well as a divine grace.

This Jesus who becomes the Christ is subject to evolution as he is subject to creation and birth. He is not made Jesus; he becomes Jesus. Trusting in the Father and exhausting his human resources in love, Jesus achieves what he might not have achieved. He saves us as someone who is no stranger to the chemistry and grain, the water and air of this planet.

Jesus, growing in the body of Mary or buried in the soil of the earth, is a new sacrament of a new mystery of unity. The unity of life is now declared not only in terms of the one God who creates or in terms of the one creative process through which we are bound to one another. Jesus brings Easter into the world, a mystery of life growing into new forms of unity.

Easter happens in the spring as the earth comes to life. It happens as a promise that the world has more to offer than first appears. God makes the world a sacrament of love; he initiates evolution as an expression of unity; he offers Easter as a communion of divine and human life. If Jesus is not lost, nothing is lost. If God's Son breathes the same air and is refreshed by the same water, grace is embedded in the earth. If this Jesus reaches the Father, not as stranger but as son and child, so do we.

4
EDEN
AND EASTER

And suddenly there is man. All the straining, reaching, aspiring of creation attain a certain finality in man. Someone who can love walks the earth. Creation senses something of its Maker in this image made of the substance of the earth and the Spirit of God. A God who loves invites someone else to love. And suddenly there is man.

Man is a promise of God made flesh; he is God's dialogue with creation made of bone and breath; he is God's way of being faithful to himself fashioned out of clay and sunlight. Man is God's exodus to a land of promise in Eden through the parting of the waters of creation, out of the darkness of chaos and the confusion of Satanic oppression. Man is God's Covenant made into a human heart, symbolized by a rainbow of promise, spoken as a Word which lives and breathes, made Adam twice over, a sacrament of Divine Presence, a cloud of fire and grace hovering over creation as the one who names the animals, shepherds and keeps his brother.

The experience of Israel and the message of the New Testament Church reveal critical aspects of human beginnings and human destiny. These insights converge with elements at the core of human life which make it distinctive: history, consciousness, freedom, and language.

Since creation is a personal process, history is essential to its understanding. Creation does not occur all at once but in a history. Its purpose is person in community.

An animal is not conditioned by that which went before it in the manner that man is. Man is compelled to reconcile himself to his own history as well as to the history of the race. An animal does not sense this need. Man reconciles himself to his own history through memory or repentance; he reconciles himself to the history of the race through the phenomenon of tradition.

An animal has no history properly speaking. An animal does what it is expected to do; it is predictable; when it modifies its behavior it does this so slightly that the change in an individual animal is not deemed worthy of historical record. In the "history" of an animal, history is not at issue. Christians are convinced that the history of one community, namely, Israel, and the history of one human life, namely, Christ's, enlighten each other and provide a unique means of interpreting human experience. In the history of Israel and of Jesus, we are given memories, reasons for repentance, and vital tradition. The meaning of these realities contain the meaning of our reality.

Man's history is critical because it is unpredictable. His unpredictability, however, is not so radical that man has creation entirely at his disposal. God has sealed a covenant with creation, a covenant which demands that life will happen only when there is love. The death of creation is the same as the death of reverence. As long as creation is managed in love, life, more and more abundantly, will flow from it.

The reasons why man is an historical animal are rooted in his consciousness and freedom. A man is who he is because consciousness and freedom are operative within him. From these forces, human history and human animality are formed into humanity. Man differs from the remainder of the creative process in his consciousness of the process and in his freedom to alter the development of that process.

The animal world also has a certain consciousness. An animal can look things over, see
possibilities, accept or reject alternatives. It cannot, however, create a history for itself because
it cannot accomplish anything wholly original
and decisively significant. Its ability, at times, to
modify its behavior and imitate human actions
depends upon its careful attention to what man
does. Man, however, does not study the animals
in order to become human in new ways. A man
can teach an animal to accomplish that which
would never have occurred to an animal had it
not been taught or trained by man. An animal
is more than itself only in the hands of man who
is more than an animal. And man is more than
man only in the grace or favor of Another who
is more than human.

An animal never interprets reality nor forms
an autonomous attitude toward it. The consciousness of an animal is nonreflective. The animal
does not know that it knows; it does not know
what it is to know; it does not know what to do
with its knowing. Because of this, an animal accepts reality and reacts to it. It cannot transform
reality or love it.

Even in its initial stages, human life differs
markedly from every other type of life. A human
child is a person before he is conscious of this

fact or free to act in a fully personal manner. A child lives and constructs his own being. No one can predict how a child will respond to reality or change it or who the child will become. From the beginning, a child is not "ours" in the same sense that an animal may be. No man is given dominion over other men. A child belongs to himself and belongs to another to the degree that he chooses.

Creation is bound to the mystery of a Word, a word given and a word kept. A human word, like human history, consciousness, and freedom, is freely experienced or else it is nonexistent. A human word is always subject to our freedom. It need not be spoken. If the word is a word of love, it cannot be spoken except in sovereign and absolute freedom. No word involves freedom more than a word of love. It offers one's personality and history, consciousness and choices to the influence and keeping of another. Because man's word of love is so free, no word he speaks is more creative. The word, furthermore, can only be delivered in self-sacrifice, with a willingness to endure death so that this word of love may accomplish itself in the flesh and heart of another.

God summons his freedom as he speaks his Word. In this freedom-keeping Word, God creates. He delivers himself even unto death if need be so that his Word of love will accomplish itself in the flesh and heart of Jesus and of the human family.

Creation is, therefore, a choice; it is not compulsion. It is freedom, not force or need. There is liberty in its every aspect. Creation is not God's effort at self-identity but donation, communion, grace, unasked for, freely given, for the sake of others rather than for the service of self. Creation is the one real choice men are ever given.

Existence is not the result of blind chance or unconcern. It is the grace of a personal act. It depends for its life and meaning on the love and freedom of someone else. Christian hope originates in the motive behind creation, in the manner and the purpose for which it was begun. Creation is God's act of love. It is not forced from God but reverently bestowed.

Suddenly, there is man. And man is a creature of history and consciousness, a subject of freedom, an object of a word of love. He alone on the earth is unpredictable and history-making. He alone is conscious of consciousness, free to restructure his experience, able to answer love with love freely given and consciously chosen. He has kinship with the animals but he alone is

God's image. God has made creation his signed covenant, his natural bond, his sealed commitment to man and with man. God has made an exodus to give man Eden, fashioned a world to make Adam, offered love to seek friendship with man in freedom.

In Christ, God himself has a history and human consciousness, freedom, and human language. In Christ, the Lord of history becomes a creature of history. The Christ of our evolving future is also the Jesus of our evolved past. In Christ, history and human consciousness, freedom and language are raised to new heights.

Jesus becomes conscious of things we might have overlooked. He chooses that which we might have set aside. He makes a history of hope, a history of Easter mornings, of life after death, of community in broken bread and healed injuries. Christ makes of human language a sacrament for communion with God, a word of celebration with one's brothers and sisters and of forgiveness for every enemy. Human language mediates a covenant of salvation by which a new Adam is sent on exodus out of the entombment of slavery back to Eden through the experience of Easter and the parted waters of death and sin. Someone must die for exodus to happen or Easter to occur. Jesus offers himself as the new lamb of freedom, as the flesh and blood of love remembered, transformed, raised to new consciousness and fuller freedom. Jesus makes his cross the rainbow of promise across the sky, heralding an Easter morning for creation after the devastation of Eden. Jesus becomes Adam twice over, shepherd and keeper, maker of man and healer of the heart. Out of clay and sunlight, not only creation and man emerge but Easter happens.

5
EARTH
AND HOMECOMING

Home is the place one starts from and seeks in return, the place for the beginning of the journey and the end of the pilgrimage. Home is the place life happens. The earth is home.

We have linked the doctrine of creation with the identity of Christ. Creation is an action in which God and the earth conspire in the making of a person. Man emerges as God's child and the earth's custodian. The core of his being, as the essence of God, is relational. Like God, man becomes himself in community. It is there that his creative power is most impressive.

Creation, made in an evolutionary framework, requires time and patience for its accomplishment. Despite the setbacks, the evolutionary aspiration upward is never decisively reversed.

Life never retreats to a lower form once a higher form has been realized. Evolution can become, therefore, an element in a Christian spirituality of hope in the future, faith and patience in the present, and commitment to progress rather than perfection. Since man is most himself in moment-by-moment progress, his salvation may be a moment-by-moment experience of discovery and growth forever.

We have considered the inner structure of human personality in the factors of history and consciousness, of freedom and language. The history man creates influences the person he becomes. The history of man's journey through time is not only a story to be told. It is also an experience to be lived; it becomes the environment in which we live, the air, so to speak, we breathe.

Israel and Jesus enter the process of history to make it new and to provide a way out, an exodus, from the confining history we may have made. Love reveals itself as the force behind creation, the point of redemption, the reality evolution aspires to attain, the core of community, the highest intensity of consciousness, the only truly free choice man makes, the essence of history, the substance of Word and communication.

Because the earth has been made as a home,
it is difficult to imagine that the earth will one
day be destroyed. Christ's promise that we shall
rise from the dead, flesh and spirit, makes it
unlikely that the earth will terminate its existence. The earth which has molded us, with
which we have worked out our identities and
encountered our limitations, the earth in which
the history of salvation runs its course, is des-
tined for transformation rather than termina-
tion. Not only Christ and ourselves but the earth
has an Easter coming to it. To maintain less
deprives creation of its solemnity. Our environment has been redeemed so that the world
mediates grace and the Presence of God in a sacramental manner.

Creation tends toward higher life, toward
love and reverence. This is creation's way of
seeking Christ and receiving Christ. A man
faithful to life in all its aspects is responsible
with the creative process and redeemed by Christ
for his fidelity. If the world one day dies, its
death, like ours, shall not signal its undoing but
its conversion into glory and further partnership
with God and man.

The New Testament proclaims the reconcil-
iation of creation with the Father. St. Paul explains that the Father "would bring everything

together under Christ as head, everything in the heavens and everything on earth" (Eph. 1, 10). "God wanted all perfection to be found in him and all things to be reconciled through him and for him, everything in heaven and everything on earth, when he made peace by his death on the cross" (Col. 1, 18-20). One day, there will be a new heaven and a new earth, a new Jerusalem. "What we are waiting for is what he promised: the new heavens and the new earth, the place where righteousness will be at home" (2 Pet. 3, 13). Creation will be transformed. "It will never be night again and they will need no lamplight or sunlight, because the Lord God will be shining on them. They will reign for ever and ever" (Rev. 22, 5). "I saw that there was no temple in the city since the Lord God Almighty and the Lamb were themselves the temple, and the city did not need the sun or the moon for light, since it was lit by the radiant glory of God and the Lamb was a lighted torch for it" (Rev. 21, 22-23).

The guarantee of creation's durability is the Christ without whom creation cannot be adequately considered. The Word of God has been declared in the history of this earth and took flesh from it. The risen, spiritual, transformative Word of God is always creative. A new heaven and a new earth will emerge, therefore, for a new man in a new kingdom. For this reason, the "in the beginning" of Genesis may be more absolute than we realize. There will never be an "in the end." Nor will God create again from nothing. The future will be one in which nothing of value is lost. The doctrine of creation, properly considered, is a foundation for Christian hope.

If this earth passes away completely, it is difficult to imagine how God's coming to us can be proclaimed as a consummation or fulfillment of the world. Evolution is not only directed toward God; it seeks its own integrity and identity. Human history and human accomplishment would not be serious and decisive events if God could establish a future for man without taking them into account. God's sovereignty over the creative process is not the same as God's setting aside the creative process.

Easter is a revelation of the future. The Father does not set Jesus aside but makes Christ rise from the human achievement of Jesus. The history of Jesus becomes the basis for the experience of Easter.

If the past and present of man are earthly, can the future be otherwise? Man cannot come home to God unless he is at home with himself.

And man is a creature of the earth as well as a son or daughter of God. The God of creation destroys nothing he makes; he purifies and transforms that which he never sets aside and never disregards.

The world gives glory to God when it becomes a home for man. As the world achieves its own glory, it celebrates the God who gave the world a glory of its own to seek. Easter is God's revelation of how much creation counts.

Home is the place one starts from and seeks in return. We began in the earth; we shall rise from the earth. Home is where life happens, created life, human life, Christian life, Easter life. The earth has been made not only for birth but also for coming home.

6
DUST
AND GRACE

There are two major philosophies in the contemporary world which explain man in a manner Christian doctrine considers insufficient. The first of these is atheistic existentialism. Such existentialism regards man as ultimately absurd and considers creation a prison from which there is no exit. The most perfect being in the universe is also the most anguished, largely because it is conscious of its unintelligibility and lack of purpose. The elements which structure the human person lead to final dissolution. Human history harbors no saving hope; consciousness is an awareness of the finality of death; freedom builds in one day that which is destroyed in the next; man converses only with those caught in the same dilemma.

The second of these philosophies is Marxism. While there are many worthwhile features of this philosophy, Marxism judges human existence capable of establishing its own order, of achieving its own intelligibility. Man builds an earthly kingdom in which salvation and meaning can be provided.

Each of these solutions misses the point as far as Christians are concerned. They discount or exaggerate human resources. The atheistic existentialist fails to account for the hunger for meaning in man; he neglects the meaningfulness which the human condition achieves and awaits. Marxism, on the other hand, tends to sacrifice the human person for the collectivity, the religious and spiritual dimensions of human life for exclusively political and economic objectives, the absolute open-ended future for a predetermined and prearranged future. Atheistic existentialism sees man as a creature of the earth alone; Marxism sees man as man's only creator. Both systems emphasize aspects of the truth but exclude other equally valid or even more urgent elements. God intended the earth as a creative process; he intended man as a community in which creation would achieve its purpose. The origins and destiny of life depend on a dialogue more expansive than that envisioned by these contemporary philosophies.

To say that man begins in a Word spoken by God is to leap into another realm of knowing. Here there is no proof. Creation ultimately demands an act of faith. Faith becomes the only means by which one learns to accept the Word of another. A Word communicates a person; and persons are not provable. One either accepts them or one does not. No one can establish his credentials as a person with someone else unless he is given faith. Atheistic existentialists and Marxists obviously live by faith. No one can survive humanly without it. The point at issue is the limits and horizons of faith. Can one believe in origins of life which go deeper than the origins and elements he sees in the earth so that God as originator is believable? Can one believe in aspects of human life which do not derive from human resources so that God is envisioned as Shepherd of being and source of love?

Creation and evolution tend toward mysticism and prayer. Creation gives no hint that higher life or further reaching, that a more expansive dialogue or a richer capacity for love are not possible. With the emergence of man, however, faith becomes a new imperative for growth.

With man, evolution demands as a condition for ascension a dialogue with realities man cannot see. The environment for growth and grace become synonymous.

The difference between Christians and atheistic existentialists or Marxists does not concern whether the earth must be enriched or the quality of human life enhanced. It is a difference of how much faith for the accomplishment of these objectives can be placed in realities man neither comprehends nor controls. This does not require that man become credulous, naively fideistic. Human life, however, continually reaches junctures where one is asked to rely on what he cannot see so that the next step may be taken. Whether this reliance assumes that life derives from a previous Love and that Love draws life beyond itself into new levels of intensity and dialogue is the point at issue. Does faith mean more than time for the character of man's future?

The measure of creation may not be taken by algebra or chemistry or even by the human equation. The cross of Christ and the Easter event are compelling sacraments inviting man to relate to the unseen as a means of transforming the earth.

Christian theology begins with the fact that man is simultaneously the dust of the earth and the image of God. The earth comes to life in his heart; and God becomes a new community through him. From the essence of the earth, God has raised up in tenderness a being for dialogue with him. Easter is a dramatic instance of the same intent.

When man speaks, God listens. He hears in man the voice of the earth and the speech of a brother; he hears also his own Word. Man speaks to God from the earth and hears God in the earth since creation is a syllable of that Word which is earth-bound as well as God-generated.

Man's union with the earth is not violent or artificial. He has not been exiled to the earth as some Graeco-Roman thinkers maintained. Rather, he was made from the earth for the earth. Nor is man's vocation to God disharmonious. God is the source of the faith and the originator of the mystery without which he cannot have sufficient dialogue. Man is made to measure the earth with the immeasurable grace of God, to sound the human heart with one Word and enlighten creation with the brilliance of love.

Man is a partner with God without parallel on earth. The new heaven and the new earth derive from his accomplishments. He makes something else of God's life as a child makes something else of the life of his parents. Man is, furthermore, radically distinct from the animals although he springs from the earth. The alliances man fashions in his flesh are unique and so remarkable that his immortality cannot be easily discounted. The New Testament faith in the risen Christ stresses the fact that man's body must live again if his spirit is to become all it must.

Christmas and Easter are the liturgical expressions of the dignity of man's flesh and the inextinguishable character of his spirit. It is not inconsistent to discover that the central ritual action of the Christian community is a celebration of the mystery of the flesh, of the body and blood, of Christ. The breaking of the bread, like the breaking of man's body in death, leads to new life. Creation, like bread, is meant to be broken, not for destruction but so that the seed dying in the earth might bear more abundant life. Easter is Christmas redone for further living. Death is birth re-enacted for fuller transformation.

Creation is a Eucharistic experience, a Paschal moment in which a lamb is slaughtered but only to give grace, in which the death of Christ's birth as one of us in Christmas is made the means of the birth through his death at Easter

so that we might be one with him. Creation is
an experience of harmony, between what man
sees and does not see, between animal life and
divine grace, between Christmas and Easter.
Like two pieces of broken bread, it is mended
not by being put together as it was but by becoming the source of higher life in a unity
beyond its own resources. This cannot occur unless bread ceases to be what it was and becomes
part of what it was not.

The atheistic existentialist and the Marxist
are not wrong in wanting to mend the world or
to restore man in all the places where he is
broken. Christianity, however, with faith in
Easter and a passionate love for creation is pre-
mised on the hope that it is not enough to heal
the wounds. Jesus with all his injuries healed is
not yet Christ. Christ happens when Jesus is
made something he was not before, when he is
vitalized by the Spirit, not of his making, in a
new way.

The earth has never been barren. From its
agony, man is born. Creation shall never be fu-
tile. Like broken bread, it will nourish higher
life. One could not take bread unless he believed
in its ability to transcend itself as wheat and
enter into the fiber of our flesh. Nor can one be
strengthened by creation unless he has faith in

its ability to transform itself from dust to grace and become a broken Eucharistic symbol of a Love even deeper than the love of men for one another.

7
SPIRIT
AND MATTER

A Christian is convinced that somewhere along the way God intersects with the development of life and graces it with humanness. How God does this and when are questions no one answers surely. But a Christian knows that something of God's life exists inside him and that this has much to do with his humanity. As with so much in life, it is not always easy to detail the changes which occur or at what point they make their influence felt. Indeed, the most profound changes are those brought about by imperceptible forces. At what moment is childhood over and adolescence born? When is a man no longer young or a woman unable to conceive further life? Who can say how innocence dies or the circumstances under which grace is given or love allowed to reign?

There are those who believe that the intervention of God in the creation of life is dramatic and determinable. At a certain moment, one process is over; God takes created matter and breathes new life into it so that now a man is born. All of a sudden, man is aware and free; he hears and responds; he reaches for God and for his fellow men; he is filled with human life and senses his distance from the animals he dominates. Those who suspect that God made human life in such a manner cannot be refuted. It may have occurred as graphically as this description depicts it.

More likely, however, is the possibility that God did not intervene in the creative process at some point but at every point. God allows matter to develop its inner dynamism at a suitable pace and in accord with its own nature. He endows matter, however, with the capacity for human life when it achieves a certain complexity and balance. God is, therefore, responsible for the emergence of human life. Matter is provided with the grace of its own transcendence when it achieves an appropriate degree of perfection. God begins rather than interrupts a process; in any case, matter alone is not a sufficient explanation for the emergence of the spirit.

This close relationship between matter and spirit in the origins of human life is paralleled in the completion of human life. Man cannot be immortal unless his flesh shares this prerogative. The resurrection of the dead is not the grotesque event it is sometimes pictured to be by painters or even preachers. It is rather an harmonious expression of unity. As matter generates spirit in the beginning, spirit generates matter in life everlasting. The development of one principle in man is always performed in virtue of the other.

Since the purpose of Revelation is not data but commitment, the point of the biblical account of human origins is the fostering of love between God and man and the increase of love among men themselves. This is the source of human life. This love is the principle according to which human life develops. In loving God, man loves his own life which derives from God. God's love makes man sacramental by sealing his spirit with the symbol of flesh and blood. Man is God's permanent sacrament; for this reason, he will always be more than spirit.

Spirit and matter do not exist side by side. They develop together, not in the sense that one cannot survive without the other but in the sense that each is incomplete without the other. In the beginning, matter exists without the spirit but it is in tension for the generation of the spirit from it. In death, spirit survives without flesh but it is in tension for the generation of the body from it. Man is not an animal who is sufficient without spiritual existence nor an angel who is complete without a body. Human life cannot accomplish its task or establish its identity without a unity of matter and spirit.

In many cases, the implications of this truth as a basis for Christian life have not been explored. The spirit is not more important than the body of man; it is merely different. One cannot degrade the body without despising man or set man's body free if his spirit is held in bondage. The spirit of man is not independent of matter since its destiny is not existence apart from matter or above matter. It seeks to possess man's body from within and to submit to it. The spirit is, therefore, not free nor itself as long as man's body is not all it should be. As long as man's body is subject to decline and death, the spirit of man is not fully redeemed.

There are alternatives, we have said, in considering the birth of man's spirit. If God intervenes directly, he is the immediate cause of the spirit's existence. Some envision this direct and immediate intervention as occurring not only in the origins of the human family but even in the creation of every human life today. The other possibility we alluded to seems more in keeping with the mystery of evolution, the relative autonomy of the creative process, and the dignity of God. God does not directly intervene but provides for the emergence of the human spirit by vitalizing matter in this direction. The human spirit would not be limited to the properties of matter any more than a sacrament is limited by the material conditions which structure it. When matter achieves an appropriate degree of perfection in the womb, the spirit of man emerges.

This explanation of the emergence of the human spirit will include the possibility of a laboratory creation of human life. If man can reproduce exactly the organization of matter which God has allowed as a precondition for the spirit, there is no reason why this reality would not be human nor why one could maintain that God was not responsible for such life. Whether this experiment should ever occur and whether the emerging person would be psychologically and emotionally sound is a question to be dealt with elsewhere. Ethics may forbid that which is technologically feasible.

God creates a world in motion, not only in cosmic motion but in life motion. This world continues to be created by God and seeks as its goal not the refinement of matter but the transformation of matter into love. Creation strains to become something above and beyond that which it is already. Its insufficiency, its desperation for life is a prayer and a plea for grace. Grace is the donation of more life when life is starved and thirsty for increase.

Christmas and Easter, the Incarnation and the Resurrection, the Eucharist and the Eschaton are varied aspects of the same doctrine. Jesus is human because his human spirit emerges from the matter of his body in the Incarnation; his victory over death is a human victory because his spirit is harmonized with his body in the Easter Event. The Church is a human community because the Spirit is bestowed upon it in the consecration of the Body and Blood of Christ. Salvation is a human experience because the resurrection of the body and life everlasting are the same thing.

8

RETURN
TO PARADISE

Eden begins Easter because creation rises to new life. Dawn is the beginning of sunrise. The cosmos is Christo-centric.

Christians consider Christ in universal terms. Christ is not proclaimed as something more but as the heart of it all. He is not an asset but the essence. It is not this or that person alone who is at issue in Christ but history and the future, meaning and life.

Some quarrel with this absolute interpretation of Christ but Christianity presents itself as decisive rather than as an arbitrary or accidental alternative. To conclude that other religious experiences are, therefore, of lesser account would be as erroneous as affirming that other children are less important because one's own are decisive.

The most enriching of human experiences is the discovery of relationships where one did not suspect they existed. A scientist is most effective when he finds harmony or similarity which no one else had discovered. A child becomes more personal as he encounters experiences which he recognizes as related to himself. Love is the celebration of unity where one did not expect to come upon it. Baptism and the Eucharist are the two most important sacraments because they initiate and structure community.

The Christian doctrine of creation proclaims the unity of the universe. The message reveals inexhaustible sources of unity, undiscovered connections, unsuspected similarities, unrealized relationships. The unity is so total that it is infinitely indivisible. Every diversity we see for the first time somehow becomes a new harmony when we look at it the second time.

Creation and Christ, the first day and Easter, the making of Adam and the Pentecost origins of the Church, Eden and the Eucharist, the separation of the waters, the freedom of Israel, and the sacrament of Baptism are united. When one separates these realities he misses aspects which become clear in their union. Evolution is a symbol of Easter when one knows how to read the signs of the times.

A Christian is someone who finds connections people miss. This is the apostolate of the Church. When one learns how to live a common life with his adversary, when he heals into oneness religions or cultures, patterns of thought or life-styles, he achieves harmony in a world desperate for mutual recognition. No one wishes to go unloved, unseen, unrelated to the larger issues and the people who might love him. Deep in the human heart there is a hunger for union with the seas, kinship with the air, the flight of birds, the unfolding of flowers, the bursting open of wheat, the brilliance of stars, the glow of light in the heavens. The rhapsody of mystical communion which man senses with the earth, with the human family, with the mystery of absolute Love is not rhetoric. It is the perception of belonging, the sense of oneness, not yet achieved or understood but already present.

Eastern religions contemplate the oneness of creation on levels Christians frequent less often. This silent sense of cosmic communion is congenial to Christianity. There is grace upon the waters, Spirit in the wheat, a Presence in the wine, life in the tomb, heaven beneath the surface of the soil. No person is a total stranger to those who lived before nor unrelated to anyone who lives now nor separable from those about to be. Death is a phase of life, not its denial; each living thing reveals man to himself; God is the One whose creation seems diverse because we see it partially rather than in one moment of full recognition. To comprehend the range of unity in its completeness would make man perish in joy and love. It would relate him to so much and to so many that the sheer excess of relationships would shatter the poverty of his heart.

God is the encounter with Someone who heals the joyful brokenness into a renewed oneness. The heart of man, exhausted in love and relationship, is restored and resurrected, graced and gifted so that it can live in new harmony. This is the meaning of bliss, the point of salvation, the purpose of heaven, the essence of ecstasy.

The message of Jesus strikes us as paradoxical because he deals with relationships on levels we have not reached. Where we had suspected contradictions, he is conscious of continuity. Paradoxes are revelations of unity where we could not see it.

God and man become one in Christ; Calvary and Easter are sustained by the same Person; the most rejected of all becomes the source of the most intensive community. The Paschal Event is an act of love achieved in opposites. The Spirit emerges from the broken body of Jesus, the victory of God is expressed in suffering denial, the bewildered disciples become persuasive witnesses, love converts opposites into members of the same body.

The first week of creation is a study of union from disparate realities. God makes man, the sand comes from the sea, spheres of light are set in the darkness, Eve differs from Adam, Eden is an environment separate from man. The harmony is perceived by God and judged good. It is only when man uses one element against the other that the peace of creation is disturbed. It is only when man sees death as the enemy of life and becomes anxious about living forever, only when man imagines God as his opposite, when the serpent and the tree of knowledge become weapons against Love, that creation suffers and is diminished.

God puts the pieces together in a new form and foreshadows the Eucharist and Eden in the mystery of Eden. He becomes the serpent of salvation in the desert of man's aloneness, the tree of knowledge on the hill of the Skull. East of Eden Easter is proclaimed when man puts creation to death because he could not perceive its harmony. Outside Jerusalem the Risen Christ

comes to life when man puts Jesus to death
because he could not grasp the relationship between God and man. Creation begins with life
and perishes in the banishment from Eden;
Jesus dies on the cross and lives in the return to
Eden on Easter morning.

EASTER AND CHRIST

The previous reflections on the relationship of Creation and Christ require further thought concerning the person of Christ. No moment is more crucial than the days from the Last Supper to Easter in establishing this identity. The process of Creation and the experience of Easter complement each other.

9

MEMORY
AND AMNESIA

Memory is a way of touching someone. On certain days, with selective mementoes, by significant words, memory is incarnate. Memory is presence seeking a sacrament or symbol in which it may be expressed. Memories and symbols continue the excess of meaning when a life too expansive for one lifetime to exhaust is lived. Amnesia and death easily become the same reality. To forget is to take away the capacity life retains to survive in memory.

Memory shared is community begun. Community is corporate incarnation of memory; it lives by tradition which is an incarnation of the past. A community creates symbols for the same reason a person does—because symbols concretize

the elusive or because symbol gives memory a
reality apart from us as the one remembered
once had a reality apart from us. Symbols become communion when they are given and
received.

The substance of memorable living is knowing the right things to say and the proper things
to be for others. Creation is memorable when it
expresses itself correctly. It forever makes sounds
and melodies, music and waves, winds and thun-
der in its effort to say the right things so that it
will not be forgotten. Every person is involved
in the same endeavor. Christians believe that
Christ is the one in whom creation finds its most
effective voice. He is also the one in whom man
learns how to speak and become unforgettably.

More urgent than speaking words is expressing them with our flesh. Speaking is most memorable when we touch the words.

The Last Supper is an effort at finding the
right words, an appeal to be remembered, a symbol by which memory is incarnated. Memory
becomes bread so that memory may be touched.
The sounds of spring become Easter so that presence may become personal and permanent. The
season of creation is the season of Christ in symbols of presence and memory, in evenings of
bread and wine, in mornings of sunrise and

empty tombs. Memory is what makes the winter wine of Christ's bleak death into a wedding song of Easter. The best of all memories, the most tender of all words converge in the experience from the breaking of the bread to the unsealing of the grave. In these memories and words, Jesus becomes a presence echoed in our flesh, resonant with nourishment and refreshment.

At Cana, Jesus gives wine as a symbol of concern so that the joy of union and need endure as a sacrament of belonging. A ministry begins at Cana in songs of celebration. Cana is a marriage sealed in wine for the creation of new life. It is a miracle which also leads to death since it begins the long journey to the cross. About to shed his blood, Jesus expresses himself again in new wine. The ministry begun in the symbol of wine is brought to a close in the sacrament of wine. The songs of celebration are now Palm Sunday singing and Paschal music. Despite the joy, death is in the air and symbols of hope and memory are sought. When those we love can no longer hold on to us, we give them something to keep so that they may yet touch us. Now the symbol is so effective, the need to be remembered so strong that the wine gives out, as it did years before, and becomes a permanent sacrament of belonging in which creation is consecrated, Christ is touched, and we are trans-figured.

When Christians assemble in memory, these reflections are activated and impart a presence. Through them, creation is interpreted. There is a joy and a terror in the remembering. A world is coming to an end and yet the supper is shared in hope. The center does not hold and yet we shall remain. Why else ask us to remember and repeat this act of love? Death presses in on every side and yet an exodus, a way out, is believable.

Death learns a new vocabulary in the language of the cross. The suffering of creation communicates a new meaning through crucifixion. This agony is the necessary consequence of love rather than punishment for living. God suffers in the creation he makes because he loves in the creation he has given. Love is the voluntary experience of becoming vulnerable. Christ on the cross symbolizes in his wounds the suffering demanded, even from God in love. The only one who suffers no longer is the one who has ceased to love.

This earth is filled with life and pain because love is present to it in so many different ways. Suffering begins with the sun and the waters; it assumes new forms in Eden because love is manifest more fully. The agony of creation is not only the anguish of loving but the awareness of not having loved enough. Creation tries to love more, to become more, and is bruised and buried in the process. Creation is a sign of the divine pain suffered when infinite love becomes infinite yearning and endless exposure to otherness. Those who suffer for the right reasons, the martyrs and prophets of love, are honored in the Christian community because the yearning of God has found expression in their hearts and words, in their tears and dying.

If the law of creation and the presence of Christ are not exempt from suffering, modern man must not be protected from it. Modern man does not suffer enough in the right causes; his security wastes him. Hope exists in direct proportion to how much one can be hurt. The cross is the central symbol of hope.

The Church seeks too much the absence of pain and the mirage of security. It keeps getting to Jerusalem too quickly. It must remain longer in the desert where suffering will make it vulnerable enough to pray and love and forgive. Creation is a long journey through the wilderness of evolution and darkness, through the desert of reverses and the struggle to survive to the making of human life. The Church is on pilgrimage through the apparent waste of human tears and wounds to the making of Christ. It must not get to Jerusalem too quickly or else it will arrive with insufficient life. Nor must it abide in Jerusalem too long while so many are on the road. Jesus is born outside Jerusalem; he dies outside Jerusalem; he is glorified outside Jerusalem. The wall of security around the city and the rock before the tomb are made of the same substance.

Jesus is alive on the cross in pain and love; those in Jerusalem do not see him. What does he do on the cross? He becomes vulnerable; he prays; he loves; he forgives. He tries to keep connections alive so that life can happen from his pain. He suffers to give rather than to take away; creation suffers for the same reason. Jesus suffers in making connections—with the Father, his executioner, the betrayer, the future, those he loves. No one gives life while he is too protected.

What does the suffering of Christ do for creation and for us? It gives us a different set of memories so that we can read creation and history right. It teaches us what to say and become so that we can be present as we ought to be.

No one reads Jesus or creation properly unless he has suffered and learned to give life through the pain. Without injustice endured, the trial is read too quickly. Without the twisting of one's words and meaning, we miss the point of the accusations. Without the injury of someone who used friendship against us, we do not comprehend the greeting in the garden. Those who remain in Jerusalem are protected from the ache and the necessity of the journey but Jerusalem becomes Egypt for them. For some, the crucifixion is a secular event, the trial is someone else's trial, Christ is an accident of history, a convenient symbol, someone to remember in security. Some build a sanctuary from his affliction, a closed Church from his open tomb.

God is in pain because he is powerless to prevent the pain which comes from love. Our amnesia must never erase the memory of God's desolation. The God we meet on the cross, like the man we meet in creative suffering, is like no other person we meet.

The suffering of Christ gives creation a new vocabulary. We do not speak as much in the desert as we do in the city but we say more. No one speaks much around a child in excruciating pain but there is more of everyone in each word. Conversation is difficult beneath the cross; but, after the sharing of pain, we never talk the same way again. Our memories are scarred with insecurity and vulnerability but vital and open to love. We get no attacks of amnesia after Calvary. We fear security when even God does not have much of it. The city is no place to be. So we go out and take our place by the cross if we have any decency or love left. And we suffer with someone dying for the sake of his life and our life. It's wrong to have no painful memories.

Jesus never said less, or more, than he did on the cross. He learned the right things to say in the shedding of his blood and the naked insecurity of his death. If we suffer enough, we learn how foolish it is not to forgive and we know how little time there is for healing and for love.

Every time we see someone die we watch our security slip away. There is hope in this, nonetheless, because God once died and left us memories of life. If God had not died on our hands, we might have sought security in the tree of knowledge supposing we could become like God without the experience of death.

10
JERUSALEM
IN THE SPRING

There is so much life in life, so much hope and joy. Creation is sown with pain and confusion, sinewed with tears and distress. But life is much more. Winter is only one season, a season with its own beauty, a season which needs spring so that it can be winter. Life has such a hold on this planet, sure roots in our flesh.

Jesus died on this planet, not because death is good in itself, but because his life cannot reach everyone until he has undergone death. In death, he gains and grows, hovers over the earth as a perennial Spirit of Easter, a bright harbinger of spring. No one is fully alive until he has gone to his limits. This is one reason why we die. The road to sorrow and joy must be exhausted so that a city not built by human hands, seated on a mountain, may open its gates. Jerusalem happens in the living out of limits, at the end of the journey, when one has crossed the boundary of the desert. Evolution and Easter are a bursting of the limits. Grace brings the death which breaks life open to the air of newness.

Hope lives through the winter in the vision of spring. Earth hopes in the Easter light of promised resurrection. Those who behold what has not come to pass allow life to grow in the present. The Church has hope from those who offer visions and dreams.

There are ministries of hope as varied as the dreaming permits. Three of these ministries are pivotal.

Hope may be shared in telling the story of creation and of Christ, in the ministry of teaching, the revelation of a sacred tradition. Tradition is life, not doctrine alone. It is life written in Scripture, celebrated in liturgy, harbored in community. To tell the story of the earth or of Jesus is to give life when the one who relates it has been reached by it. The mother who loves her deceased husband is the only one competent to tell the story of his life to her child. Her husband comes to life in her memories and words because she loves him and because she loves this child. Tradition must not be entrusted to those who love the past and mistrust the present nor to those awed by venerable words but impatient with people. They alone bring life out of a story, tradition out of the past, who love the earth whose story they tell and reverence Christ in people.

Hope may be shared in the anger of protest or the force of prophecy. The prophet bears life as he witnesses against the abuse of life, the abuses of a verbal interpretation of the life of Christ, the abuses of society or the Church, the way men deal with one another or handle creation or infect history with fear. A story may be told with fire and accusations, delivered in rage: "This earth has been made for life and you have laid it waste"; "This is the house of God, the Church of Christ, and you have made it a den of thieves and liars."

The prophet is marked for death. He protests against the enslavement of life even as his life is taken from him. The crucified body of Jesus is a protest against the machinery of the State and the machinery of the Church, a protest against Rome and Pharisaism, against secular and ecclesiastical Caesars. Pentecost is born in the burning of the Spirit and the prophetic preaching of those who, inflamed by courage, live no more by fear. "God raised up him whom you judged evil. We have seen. We are witnesses ready to die in our prophecy against you."

Hope may be shared in telling the story by one's style of life. Everyone who is happy is a rebel in an unhappy world. In contemplation, one becomes in his flesh a memory of Jesus, an incarnational hope, consecrated in the style of life he lives, effective merely because he is present, persuasive with his living and his heart. He makes community happen not because of his teaching or prophecy but because he enters your life.

Life takes root in pain and the memory of suffering. Jesus dies and we hold on to hope. Life is given only when the bread is broken, the wine drained. A *plus* is more than any number of *minuses* in the equation of life; one Easter cancels out all the Calvaries; one spring flower marks the end of winter.

Those who go through the right experiences know what to say and be for others. When the Church says the wrong thing, it reveals the fact that it has not undergone the right experiences. The disciples knew what to say and become in Pentecost because they had died a thousand deaths in the days before and were willing to sustain a thousand more in the future. They told the story of creation and of Christ in teaching, protest, martyrdom. They told the story with their flesh and blood and they told it so well we call it Scripture. One tells the story of creation or of Christ properly not because he uses an approved catechism but because he has undergone the right experiences. The orthodoxy of the Church is not a question of rote or rhetoric; it happens when the Church goes into the desert, outside the city, to die on the cross and hope for Easter from resources not its own.

Any season of the year is nearly Easter. Spring is a permanent word of hope. It always comes. It cannot be halted. No matter how long or fierce the winter, spring forces its way through the tons of ice and snow. Creation never dies nor does Christ nor do we. After all the savage cold and shattering wind, the earth grows green with hope; and flowers so fragile they could not be touched force their way through the darkness of the earth to the morning sun. No matter how horrible the death, how unbearable the pain or absolute the rejection, despite the tons of stone and dirt against the tomb, Easter happens and life grows green as all the forces of death are exhausted.

11
EASTER
IN SILENCE

Christ's death has something to say to every man. But the burial . . . God at the edge of the wilderness. . . . Whom do you talk to when someone you hoped in collapses and dies? Is it worth talking to anyone else again, really talking? Jesus is buried in the spring . . . just when hope was happening. The Church comes apart . . . just when we need it to hold together. On some mountains, transfigurations go on all the time. But eventually you get to the top of one of those mountains covered with crosses and tombs, no God to talk to, only a graveyard. How do you recover when someone you hoped in dies beyond recovery? The same earth that gives us spring covers Christ.

God never stays long where things function

smoothly. God gets impatient with a Church that gets it right too often. After someone goes through Good Friday, he never trusts things that function smoothly. There is no silence like the silence of someone you once talked to and recently buried. There is no darkness like that first second after the candle is extinguished. Darkness seems easier when no candles are lighted; silence appears more bearable when there never was communication. When someone you loved is buried, you try not to care, as a defense, because death only hurts if you care.

The most difficult of all times are the in-between times. Something is gone and nothing new takes its place. No one knows what to do with Holy Saturday; it is the only day of the year which has no liturgy. But Jesus talked of memory and words. If we do not talk about the one who is gone, he is gone forever; if we do not remember, he is no longer present to us. It takes so much hope to talk again. The worst death is the death of becoming silent not because words would spoil the happiness but because you know it will do no good.

Communication dies in security. Danger makes people talk the way nothing else does. Perhaps Jesus is buried to take away our security. Scripture is what the disciples shared with one another when they no longer had Jesus nearby. Security keeps talking, loving, remembering, hoping from becoming all they must.

The more security we have the more frightened we become. With the most powerful weapons in history, we become insecure. When we had a secure Church, we feared more people than we do today: non-Christians, other Christians, Communists, birth-control advocates, public school systems, secular newspapers, divorced and remarried couples, those who missed their Easter duty.

We find it difficult to talk when we wish to own the people we meet. It takes time and love and pain to learn that everyone is on loan, that no one stays very long, not even Jesus.

Somehow spring knows it is going to die. Every year, however, it talks its heart out because summer is already the beginning of winter. When we know how short the time is, we say well what we want to communicate. When we sense we are all on loan, we realize how absurd it is not to talk and forgive.

We never owned Jesus or one another. When a person is gone, the memories and words get deeper inside us. Perhaps this is why they must go away. If spring never came again, we would treasure its final passing; as long as we are certain it will return soon we hardly see it. Life tells us that there is always someone to talk to but there is never anyone to own.

Some in the Church waste time trying to own Jesus, to keep him in their corner. Our corner, however, is his tomb. Keeping someone in our corner is another way of burying him. We waste so much life in the Church trying to own those over whom we suppose we have authority. People do not wish to be owned, merely talked to and allowed to go free.

Jesus hated being owned. Nor did he wish to be an owner. When some tried to make him a king, he walked away a little disgusted. But when people came to talk, he had hours to spare. Nicodemus spent all night talking.

Creation was meant to be a place where communication would go on all the time. It was never made to be secure; even Eden was not safe. Creation was supposed to be an in-between time, a pilgrimage, with no one to own nor any settled city. The Tower of Babel was one of those foolish attempts to make something permanent out of clay and water. We suffocate life every time we act as though it were made for us to own. Every year spring is buried as a reminder that no one owns it.

Silence breaks the heart in a million pieces.

We create hope by our conversation. Hope dies when people never answer or play games with words.

Jesus is buried in the spring, as the wheat waves in the wind and the grapes grow rich on the vine. Jesus is buried in the Passover season, a sign that he will pass over into our hearts where the memory will endure and the words will be written in our flesh. It all has to happen inside us now. The top of the mountain is never a graveyard if the spirit of man is transfigured. Cana no longer requires earthen jars if there are human hearts and hopes. Easter is given to those who realize they do not own Jesus and who lose a grip on their security. The dead bury the dead; the living are too busy bringing them back in memories and words. Jesus is buried in the spring but he rises into every community which remembers him and communicates in love.

There is a great difference between having no one to talk to and not knowing what to say. Despair begins when we sense we no longer belong to the people we thought were on our side. We become speechless when we discover those we thought were indifferent to us. A Christian is most successful when people find it difficult to know what to say in his presence. Jesus had this effect on people. The woman taken in adul-

tery did not know what to say before Jesus. The
woman who anointed his feet was startled by his
acceptance. The prodigal son rehearsed his
speech but could not deliver it when he found
himself in his father's arms halfway through the
sentence. Zacchaeus and the Samaritan woman
were touched with joy beyond speaking by the
unexpected part Jesus had in their lives. John
relates how difficult it was to speak when the
disciples saw Jesus on the shore soon after Easter.

Paul becomes an apostle when he experiences
his belonging to someone he persecutes. He later
writes of belonging the way no Christian has before or since. He repeats often his message on
the Body of Christ, the fact that all, all are one.

John XXIII once greeted a party of rabbis
with the words "I am Joseph, your brother." It
was difficult to speak after such a reminder of
belonging.

One reason why we become startled into joy
by belonging is the awareness that there is more
to us and to life than we suspected. We become
speechless because we need silence for the mystery. Christianity confesses that we are children
of infinity. We never stop growing. Heaven happens as we find forever how much we belonged
to those we never knew.

This is the vision Jesus had for the Church.

It was a great idea. It still is. The great ideas in the Church are not in the doctrine but in the belonging. This is also the lesson of the Judgment and the end of creation. We continue to live if we sense how much we belong to those who need us. In a sense, we live in their need. The one who is his brother's keeper recognizes the Father of so many sons and daughters.

The last place the Jewish rabbis expected to find Joseph was in Rome and as Pope. The first time Joseph was in Egypt. Joseph keeps turning up unexpectedly. The discovery never loses its appeal. This is what life is all about . . . finding your family.

Mary of Nazareth discovers a family and a son in Jesus. She becomes frightened and does not know what to say because there was so much belonging in the relationship. Those who keep his words become not only mother but father and sister and brother to him. The Last Supper is the making of a family. We share the same flesh and blood, memories and hopes. We have a common tradition in our communal life. "I'll not leave you orphans." When Philip becomes excited and asks for the Father, Jesus says in effect: "Philip, where have you been? I'm your father and your brother. It's all one."

God tells us who he is. You only reveal yourself to your family. Creation is an act of revelation, a home to make a family in, a place to look for Joseph. The more we grow the more we realize how similar we are to each other. The common core at the heart of different cultures, the unifying experiences at the center of diversified centuries, the repeated themes in the world's great religions, the shared history among the many races of the earth remind us of our one origin and one destiny. Christianity is not at its best when it explains the difference it makes but when it shows how little difference there is.

The Last Supper is an effort at making a family and creating a communal awareness, a revelation or insight into brotherhood. Jesus did this so well in his appeal to be remembered, in his consecration of creation in bread and wine, in his establishing kinship in the communion of the same flesh and blood, in his promise of a Spirit for those who compose the same family, that the Supper became the one action of Jesus the disciples kept repeating. The disciples discover their identity in this action of Jesus; they continue to learn through it those to whom they belong, their common Father, their unknown brothers and sisters.

The Church is a process of belonging. We have the same mother and father, the same flesh and blood, the same brothers and sisters. We were raised on the same words. Every spring creation comes alive for us the way it did when first it was made. Every Easter we are reminded that creation is on the side of life and that we were made to give life to one another. A family exists so that those in it can offer life to one another. Jesus had a great idea for the Church; the Father had a great idea for creation. It's all one. You learn that or you learn nothing.

It seems so wrong to try to exclude people. Some in the Church waste their lives condemning, emphasizing differences, obsessively judging others less worthy than they suppose themselves to be. While some are busy attacking others so that their Church can be safe, secure, comfortable, Jesus is washing their feet. He never was very good at keeping people out; he brought in Samaritans and Roman centurions, public sinners and well-known prostitutes, the poor and the blind, a few lepers, and an executioner or two. Someone in the Church is always around following his example by opening windows just when we finished dusting off the riffraff.

The Church begins when Jesus, with tears in his eyes, gets a basin of water and then asks his friends to share the bread he was eating and to understand how difficult it was for him to know what to say because the time for leaving was so near. He was leaving and he wanted the belonging to continue. He yearned to take them with him. He got as far as the Garden and then they left . . . after all that talk about belonging. On Easter, he tried again; he was first seen in the Garden looking for them; it was Eden again. "Mary . . . Rabbi." Silence. It's difficult to know what to say.

On the cross, Jesus ached to belong, begged not to be cut off, asked the Father not to forsake, the disciples not to forget. He tried to call us out of the city, away from Jerusalem, because there were too many people on the road who needed us. When you are dying, you remember the names of those who belonged to you. Even a child remembers the names of those he cannot do without. Jesus does the same and dies while calling his Father, his mother, his son, his brother with the hammer in his hand, and his brother with the nails in his hands and feet. He makes the Church so that no one would feel homeless, unwanted, unthought of, condemned, rejected, of no worth. It's all on loan. Why not heal before the light goes out and the darkness of death takes away the time we were given?

Christians are obliged to talk about belonging. It's the only way to get Jesus out of the tomb

... and all creation with him. Jesus does not come back because it's Sunday morning ... that would be a foolish reason to return. He comes back because there is a community to return to, made up of those who know they belong to one another. His disciples are those who love one another. What is the point of leaving a tomb if you have nowhere to go, if you no longer belong? What is the point of having a Church if no one feels he really belongs to it or it to him? Why have a family which belongs to no one?

Easter morning is described with so few words. Mary apparently said nothing. Peter and John did not know what to do so they ran out to check the tomb. They remind us of a mother who cannot sit still and talk when her son returns because of her joy. She runs around doing a lot of useless things because she does not know what to say. When the sense of belonging is rich and overwhelming, no one remembers what to say or what he said. There is a silence and a peace at Easter as there will be in the fulfillment of creation. It is not a case of having no one to talk to but of belonging to so many and caring for them so much that it becomes difficult to know how or where to begin.